SEA OF

SELECTED POEMS 1972 - 1989

DIANA DURHAM

WITH DRAWINGS BY CATHERINE SMEDLEY

THE DIAMOND PRESS

To Michael and Nancy, pole stars and friends.

To Jon, for his love and surround.

To Jay, for his vision and encouragement.

To Maria, for friendship in strange places.

CONTENTS

'And I saw as it were a sea of glass mingled with fire; and them that had gotten the victory over the beast, and over his image, and over the number of his name, stand on the sea of glass, having the harps of God.'

Revelation 15 v 2

'And he measured the wall thereof, an hundred and forty and four cubits, according to the measure of a man, that is, of the angel.

And the building of the wall of it was of jasper: and the city was pure gold, like unto clear glass.'

Revelation 21 v 17-18

1 Prelude

Unknown men wrought huge megaliths
Into majestic computers
Angled to coincide with the sun and moon.
They stretched out their arms in worship
To the sky, and the eyes of the sphinx
Stare eastward still in eternal
Anticipation of the sun's light

MALCONTENT

Sitting absently in a lesson, listening
In politely, the corner of a window catches
The eye, and thoughts stroll through
To mount the clouds: a grey ridge laced
With gold straddles the chasm of the sky where
Rolling caravans and men cloaked with the wind
Go striding endlessly toward the orient east.
Nobly in the north a piled head of cloud
Rears up: imperial but gradually usurped
By wistful bands of chorusing blue.
Within me drives the rain through tottering
Back streets at time of dusk,
Curls the river in the roar of dawn
Demanding entrance to the ocean,
Sets the sun in a storm of colour
Giving up it's silent cry of war.

MAGNET CITY
Southend-on-Sea

Bankruptcy of Heartbreak House
Home of emotional down and outs
Hopeless rooms airless retreats
One of time's dead end repeats
House on this site for centuries
From flames, unhealthy phoenix,
Of an old man's intellect, last
Thumping of the life force beat.

Heartbreak Hotel blues
Yes just passing through
Cold motel morning, empty road
Gleams motorbike metal shine
Rough purrs like the rough rhyme
Of silver sixties Elvis -
Your style lights still tight
Glide of the American dream swan -
Poetry in motion, surfer on the wave
Fragment of the sunlit dancer
Motion of the water glister
And movie pictures move you so -
Now all scrap metal, skid row.
Rocked in your dream ship's wake
Let down by the tide and left
Stranded on the mud of Magnet City.

Headhurt Hotel, budget glamour
My heartbreak booked me in your
Sleazy surface one night long
Lonely hotel bedroom song.

Love filled the streets with wonder
Heartbeat throbbed the neon nights
Sea rushing streams - but tide
Ebbs, love turns and Apollo on
A motorbike rode out of town.

12

Old names skid through years towards me
Peter Pan's Playground, child eternally,
Electric paradise blossoming spite
With dangerous and forbidden night
Glitter toadstools spring by real trees
The Never-Never Land, hopes spree
Lights of the fairy village, childhood treat
Lights across the river, teenage cheat
Mercy cold on stark narcotic nights.

Look around from your waterfront
See the sign - Hope Hotel - O Magnet City
Prison house take off, heartburn beat,
Futures bloomed like full bellied
Spinnakers, sprung through blue skies
Falls a scattering of broken promises.

Now its poor old Apollo
Pick up the fragments, and step down
Call me Marlon, swinging off
The penny-ride real Harley
(And the little girl's face lit up
Though the reindeer was too slow)
Muddy centre golden mile
Las Vegas doughnut palace
Saxophone penguins jumble Beatle tunes
All the money machines remain unmoved.

Spreading rings of blue nights
(Wheels spark in the protest skid)
Forced up towards the stars
O night of a thousand eyes
A weekend full of stars, magic
Moments falling star catch,
He sighs unseeing on the quest.

Pick up the pebble shell bits -
Happy small time captains
Hug the coast in beer smiles,
The river and the messing in boats
Pier floats out to meet the tankers,
Unfleshing of the pink silt ripple
Low tide salmon shades and blues.

Then as we slow glide the boat
Sudden train beat shunts across
Quiet waters, vulnerable violence
Of a ship's heartbeat, pain throb
In still centre of the spreading wake.

And evening air glass distance
Flickers the lights blue shades green.

CRYSTAL GAZING

In the few rare and precious moments,
Clustered and twinkling like bright jewels,
I see dimly, through faceted crystal,
A deep light burning.
But the bauble is moved, and the light replaced
By my face, mirrored a thousand times
In lengthening distortion and turning,
The thousand faces turn with me.

Only when the gem is shattered
And the empty darkness
Scatters its stars away,
Only when the candle glow
Flames brighter, fires through
The fettering glass,
Do you find each moment
Cut into perfect synthesis
Turned through the spectrum's rainbow
But burning a constant white.

2 Fire Path

My mind is straining to catch
Some vast process of creation
Turning round to reach completion;
My form takes on new shape
And I no longer shun
What that might mean
Nor fear to lose control,
But let the changes come.
What must be, must be,
The seed must grow into the tree,
So we grow in heaven on earth
Trusting the seasons of rebirth.

A THURSDAY EVENING

Feelings fused, at ends
shorted and somehow abused
by things - the early night
of November and the neon glare -
my room seems stale, the
jewels and pictures false:
nothing glows anymore.
Littleness squirms inside me -
give way, but where to?
Tears are close, but vicious,
talk, reach some one in the night,
but he'd think female and a drag,
and she'd give a cautious, well-
judged sympathy. We don't
break out of ourselves, separate.
So I just write down and
the words smoke awhile then cool.

MUSIC THROUGH CLOSED DOORS

Sometimes music calls, filtering closed doors,
And opening, I still expect a cinderella change:
Candles flaming in tiered circles to the roof,
The elegant black tilt of men, edged with white,
And ladies in flounces of brilliant colour
Swopping curtsies and bows and witty remarks
In a balanced whirl of repartee and dance.

LONDON STUDIES

1

In the light of this grey-cloistered,
Arched and booklined catacomb,
This collect pinnacle of culture -
I seem to plumb my own Dark Ages.

Here in the gloomy shades of
Literature the dead threaten
The living, intermingle their dust,
As we the sterile body critic
Bleed old works dry, like
Ancient physicians.
We the parasites of dead
Men's minds treat their
Experience like our own:
Shakespeare deteriorating
Into bibliographies,
Our responses decaying
Into the secondhand.

2

Riding a red bus through the grey
Of a great city, I seem to find
A pattern of my mind laid out -
Sprawling in streets and
Occasional monuments
Smoke, noise and glimpses of trees.

At times the architecture blossoms,
A square draws out a street,
The street faces a templed gallery,
A statue centres the complex:
The meditational dot amidst
Petal-edged squares.

At times it slips into jumbles:
Huge roadways roar
Across huddled rooftops,
Office blocks flash high
Over any park tree, any half-
Moon of Regency proportion.

As lines of thought travel
And link, so the bus links
The huge unwieldy city -
But momentarily - round corners,
Up streets, the vision only
Partial, glinting fragments.

3

Crumbling past into present
Thought wanders fragmented,
Like city rumble, like twilight
Echoes through labyrinthine
Coils of library, like the
Sweet Thames, glinting bright
Between city walls and bridges,
Softly running now and in
The poetry of old, smoothing
Past gold into present grey.

THE PYRAMID

I have paid the price
I have sacrificed
My vision for another's.

I entered this place
Anticipating grace -
Attendant on past mysteries

I neglected my own.
(In the future shown,
Gleaming, now bedimmed.)

The eunuch am I
Complaisant spy
Of Cleopatra's beauty.

Dumb spectator
Gelded creator
Of golden silence.

I watch gold sand
Run through hands
Of the gorgeous dead.

Passages are sealed,
Eternity revealed -
Trapped, in a symbol of stone,

I watch in darkness
The poem's process,
Entombment of life in death.

BARKERS' ANGELS

Your poised and angled elfin mercy
Puts all self-pitying to shame
Service sparkles from your survey
Eyes and fingers tipped with flame
Electric strength tingles round you
Resonating tones of love.

(To the mannequins in Barkers' Christmas window display.)

DRIVE IN SOUTH WALES

Those heavy, grey-gold
Country drive scenes:
A curl of road and tree.

The still, wet fire
Of fern, trees
Emerging into skeleton above.

A dark horse's head
Frozen breath furling
Over the dulled blaze of hedgerow.

White-tipped, a stream falls
Through the arched stone bridge,
Bushes corallised on either bank.

At our approach crows
Type patterns in the air:
A faint mist, smoking

Into grey, moulds all
To winter, while a pale
Sun melts weakly through above.

CORNWALL

Crimplene Cornish ladies
loud in corner Spar stores
cloth-capped old men
stepsit, sea guardians.

Long bus rides, pasty pubs
craft and gift shops - seagulls
under glass, assorted knots
piskie spoons, polished stones,
and summer bubble culture -
California mini-marts
wave poster, T-shirt twist and
transcendence of the surfboard
porpoise-nosed like fisher boats.

A certain stern stone grey
council rows, tin mine, chapel
winter's thick flying dusk
and grey sea sky mist
dampen bamboo lanes
shine slate roofs; days
of no more people, black-
windowed farm house hid
but grey-eyed morn
chequers with light:
grass sparks light the grey
quiet mauve cabbage flow,
blue smoke bells, silver bone
pines and yellow gorze stars
red poppy flickers golden corn,
sunshine blue green fierce skies
and bright star shine on navy nights.

Noise shapes - sea rush, tree
top wind rock wave roll
gull chorus calls, stone
hurl, scream fall fill
structures of the air cliff space.

Fern spray - wave break
curl and clump of road and wood
ribbon road, hedgerow
storm tree stoop and ship
wind wild weather round
one white still horse.

Grey post telegraph wires
(sound waves, sculpture strings)
stake mist mauve moor humps
broad floating wave backs,
still and spreading, moulded by
blue air stroke, grey cloud roll
and ripple flat wide circle sea.

Night shade red danger
stars dark hung wall vine

bright bird dives between
black green tree-top crests

leaves blown back flash
white-winged bird flock

lighthouse swoops wide light wings
over troubled water surge springs.

Empty engine house cuts space
cliff top chimneys golden faced
slow by the smuggler sea ways
ocean rollers ravaging caves.

Gold glow ocean day fall
sunflower solitary garden wall
end of the day land, sun sleep rest
day-tripper deity heading west.

(Partially inspired by Barbara Hepworth's sculpture)

MORNING SEA

in the tidal wave morning
golden galleon forever sailing
over metallic blue of the heavy sea
ripple scratched into distance
gold scratched and white-tipped motion
of water flow wind driven
tree top ruffle rustles framing
of the view, above roams
wild, uncharted sky-vine blue

SUMMERWINTER

sun on rock
flies sirening
flickers of wind

turquoise sky
white pearl roofs
ice stars burn

HEAVEN AND EARTH

Light funnelling rose-shaped out of darkness
Silence rouses into shape
Gathers crouched limbs and upstands
Man, speaks the word
I am, there
At the
Cross
Over
Point, that
Focus am I
Legs straddle earth, hands touch the
Waving air, human symmetry
Cross of power, not blood, through him
Falls the rain, blows the wind, grows the earth, shines the sun.

NEW NOTES
for Oliver

the grand genius of gesture
o so sophisticated court jester
flung his hand into the sky
caught the glance of a knowing eye
store up in his velvet pocket
later in his turret took it
gazed at the stars, looked in the mirror
reflected on Mars, longed for a river
that would float him on strong
over the trauma of being wrong.

champagne princess lost her mist
for love I took the universal risk
he shouted to a silent world
the court yawned, no one heard
looking round for the diamond eyes -
(let the river in your heart arise,
open up your silken hearted door) -
couldn't sleep, paced the floor
checked it out, compared his notes
outside new note silver music floats.

POPULAR LOVE

the tiger footed tyrant love
sneaks his head around the door
lifts up blank eyes and grins
snarls in smiley dread intent
at clients clumsy with petition
the ever-hopefuls growing cold
in his shivery white-walled waiting-room.

LONDON LADIES

Young London ladies
cockney and pert
baring their teeth
with lots of s's
sharing cheap confidences
up on the tops of
red London buses.

CENTRES

Meditational dot
amidst petal-edged spheres
fierce white blank
of the unseen sun's centre.

Outer flames of the inner fire
red fierce flames of white honey focus
flicker in the serene sphere rush
wind of a still flowering radiance.

The circle loops up tighter to the centre
no windspace shows the wave's beat
all is one centred, one syllabled,
assonantal of white bright light.

CITY SONG

city oh city
of smoking stone
your pavements are jostled
litter is strewn

city oh city
of ancient stones
years press upon you
streets are left bare

city oh city
of broken stones
dark fills your vacancies
neon nights stare

city oh city
of smoking stone
heat burns at corners
melting down bone.

SUICIDE DRIVE

Rising swiftly to the pinnacle of this Parisian tower
Space expands in vast invisible shapes around.

As the tower narrows to a single point
Heavy voices of the unseen beast
Cry out above a city's multi-headed sleep,
A river's helpless twist
The past's charismic shifts
Crumble in the dry white heat
And this crazy exhibition piece
This grand wrought iron Babel
Soars recklessly to unknown
Vertical perspectives.

City rumbles gently,
The beast cries out,
The great belly in space
Heaves like a vacuum
To suck me in:

Jump - blow the line
Drop - the world's all
Lost in a second's searing fall
Gambler against God's third ace,
Ungrateful bargainer for grace.

In the cheap throw, suicide dive
And the old earth's staggering stride
Temple tops and Babylons divide -
But something holds,
On the sacred mountain's peak
Cross-over point of Zion

A thin thread
Unbroken in the desert forty days
Unbroken in the garden
Always.

TAKE OFF

Sharp London air
Controlled pell mell

People who fill you with their emptiness
People big enough to love

cradle
rock me
in the hands
of the living
drift me
float
fill me   warm   blue   bright

a slow flight
with the wings of all silver speed
a long soar
upwards

PRELUDE

I have friends
among the ruins
picking out a corner
blown by each new wind
ignoring the death of normal.

friends, still trying
to drop out somewhere,
while their blue vision vistas
of air and desert sand fill
with invisible contracts
paper money power

friends, steeling their eyes
walking up to the networks
of commitment, proud
and sensible martyrs,
iron in the soul
to hang on to

and though I may seem
to be sitting on the fence
I've been gradually
slipping off all year
and now temple doors swing
open new air rush
so I go
to never leave you

3 Return to the Temple

Quiet times, the night is tender
Inbetween dark trees, snow holds
Sparkling silence.

Something strained relaxes now
Hearts open in this starfilled night
And fall like rare snow flakes
Painful, frost white blossoms
Gentle to our touch.

SPIRAL STAIRWAY

the pattern takes shape
stairway curves upward
and beyond - beneath awaits
the next; but hands reach
from that questioning
to one above, always the
step above, the step below.

desired unfolding, spiral,
but darkness looks around
the corner, out of sight
cold air, dizzy height
no turning back, that
way the bitter taste
uneasiness of the untried.

at each new bend feels
still the life behind, fears
the unseen upward curve,
approval of the scheme, but
cold dismay curls at
repetition, reformation
endless winding of the stair.

each new break away a leap
from type to type:
tender rising to cold
of well worn stone.

but you my mentor and my guide
at once above and by my side
turn my gaze to the one below,
join up a fiery ring of power
and lighten the turnings of this tower.

A PICTURE HANGING AT EDENVALE

careless flower petal fall
water drop of muslin
light sprays into the picture
as piano notes climb
a fineness fallen to decay
petals lying over-blown
brown edges round the bloom
and in the soft fine eyes
of the pale cheeked girl
a golden shafted light
a look of ends

DELICATE PROCESS

There comes a point upon the stair
when others who were passing there
seem unconcerned to further prove
the fragile turnings and no longer move
on and upwards through the finer space,
they all seem to have run the race.
But in the intimate places of the heart
is known what other change must start -
who will that full pureness finally achieve
which the world's heart so longs to receive?

SPACES

Magician in the tall stone tower,
Apprentice to the passing hours,
Looks up from his still small place
Into the bright skies' bountiful space
And sighs a little as he weaves
Connective tissue, precious leaves
Of substance - gold-dust for a ravaged world
Carefully prepared and spun on spools,
Like silken life-lines safely stored
As mystery in the heart that soars
Within, though quiet without,
Still spinning, shining all about.

MORNING SONG

Bright shafted mornings gleam
Strong as cold-washed stone;
Noon turns tall as suns and
Colours in the afternoon weave
Rich matt tapestries of earth and leaves.

All the day's sweet fruits are bound,
Their sweetness rises on the evening blue
Like whited crests on the flooding waves -
Star seeds of the seven sweet sisters
Dipped in the cool dark seas of night.

GALAXIES

Through hollow halls of black sheen velvet
And inky dark smooth shine of jet
Faint and far off bubble cries
Of recognition slowly rise.

Through the black and streaming tide
Like stately sailing galleons ride
The golden galaxies in flight,
Bright singing starwheels of the night,
They sound strange love songs in their motion
Like mystic whales of the ocean.

TOMORROW'S SEA

Inky inlets and goldflake waves
Secret beneath the harvest moon -
Galleon sailing golden and forever
On dark sea-skies of the night.

Bedspread and blanket fields fold
Down valleys and village roofs,
Dreams come surfing through the night,
Of Christmas, stars and chimney smoke.

Curl of road and cat's eye burrows deep
Through safe-dreaming childhood country sleep.

THE CHILD'S WAY

From the sleepy comfort of familiar
well travelled old-age armchairs,
teddy bear clusters, still undespised -
the child awakes, awaits, sharp-eyed.

Through the window into darkness
through the wardrobe into snow,
through a tiny door into wonderland,
from one hundred years' slumber into love.

The older ones take much longer,
wandering around for years sometimes,
chasing damsels and dragons and the Holy Grail.
But no spell can hold back the young,
they slip through talons of the beast,
running like quick silver to their source.
They carry their secret easy back home,
and don't try explaining to the grown-ups.

GROWING UP

dear well spring
deep running river
dear heart's song
singing silver

The trees stop moving
and the train takes over

we are no longer wrapped
in swaddling complexities
of a grown-up world
waiting to discover coherence

the complexity is tangle
the knotting of conflict
the weaving has stopped
the pattern is lost -

the cut cloth unravels

at its edges

and as the world slows down

we begin to move

ALL STORIES ARE THE SAME

The story has three stages -
everyone makes the first,
some the second,
very few the last.

The single road divides:
some walk backwards
round the bend,
refusing recognition of a choice;
others stare intent ahead, but
still their feet swerve round,
and later on, old mice, they'll swear
the sacred mountains were never there.

Some say it is upon a hill
truth stands, or up a ladder:
both purgatories difficult to climb -
turn by turn, rung
by moral rung.
Few have reached the top,
fewer still reported back -
views and vistas, clean air flow -
for, like mists before the dawn,
all metaphor, all talk of mountains
and cloud-capped palaces
melts away when the vision clears.

CARIBOO
British Columbia

Caribou run
Spots on a deer's back
Galaxy stars
Run homewards
Across green empty spaces
Returning from summer
Constellations
To their winter home
Cariboo.

Islands of green mist trees
Mysterious dark and new
Free and away under the sun
Ships up-anchored in the blue.

Sunny waters
Dust and snow
Deep northern nights
Stars bright between tall trees.

Ranching land -
Innocent and large
Clean blue silver bright -
A setting.

Few layers left from former times,
Indian trails, gold dust,
Memories wiped clean,
No Old World mists
And crying ghosts.

Nights span from the North Pole
Into deepest space
Orion marching with his sword
Pleiades singing soft
Cradling the earth
Guiding our journey homeward.

COMPLEX BEYOND COMPARISON

Moonbreak above clouds
Floating free -

Oh the deep tides of night
Constancy of the changing stars,
Interlacing depth,
Whirlpools of fire
Pulsing with unending power,
Vast dimensional joyous shout -
Fiery network, spectrum of being.

We begin to see our lives
Patterned and perfect
Complex beyond comparison,
Shades of green -
Leaves   depth   movement
   Blue   purple   gold
Of green,
We wind the forest path
And burst into sunlight.

(Think of all the secret lives
Folded like a day and
Tucked into the tresses of time,
Forced and uncomfortable as petticoats.)

The earth seems smaller now,
No longer teeming with cattle and space
And cooling with the sundown.

Embrace this little globe,
Green blue gold.
Join hands around this table
No longer chasing Might
Nor fabricating Law.

We told the wrong story, gentle knight,
And, as we followed from afar,
Puzzling over marvellous deeds
And mystical ships,
Your trail was lost.

Come in on another line,
Clear-eyed Galahad,
Knight of the green glades,
Spreading pools of ease,
Shaking glints of joy,
Sun-shafted sword at side
Alert and quiet on your breathing horse.

Complex beyond comparison
Our stories weave into one.

BUTTERFLIES

Brown repeating butterfly drawers:
Rainbow collected in uniform layers.

No longer talk except in units
Singles multiplied into types
Seed pods of ideas and words
Scattered in the changing winds.

And you stand almost overcome
As the simple gateway shows
Sudden vastness of a new world
Rustling golden like ripe corn.

Be thorough in this new land
Learn the language well,
Lest you wander speechless
Through gardens of flowers
Whose names and shapes
You have not power to speak.

Let your balance rest and rise
All action bounded by depth of being,
Move in the season's patience
Stay, go or walk on through
Greening shades and water pools.

Watching grey watered reflections -
Dove wings rise from the rounded cote -
Without looking up you see again
That central stairway of ascension.

REAPER

That barren-harvest, hollow look,
Nothing but an accent and a past,
All facade and no substance -
What weariness is in you!
Even your grief is stereo-typed.

Your loves have all wounded
Worn down the soft richness,
You are a brittle shell, echoes
Emptying into the air.
You renounce love, which
You never knew, and you are dry.

Love comes from nowhere
And melts the world.

Don't you remember
Blue skies high as your vision,
Sweeping round and reaching out,
That former time of space
Reverberating inside and
Connecting with the vistas.

A time when gesture was language,
All movement grace.
The hard-won sculpture essence
In motion with the waves,
Walking with us in love.

MOUNTAINS
to Martin Exeter

As the mist of emotional hangover cleared away
it was good to look up,
and come again to the feet of the mountain,
great noble paws of the lion.

You offered a steely challenge
to all private quests, something
as definite as unseen mountains,
strange in its newness,
yet old as the hills and familiar
as all the green myths which grow
and die in the hearts of men.

Beginning to know your spirit
is to express the same, to climb higher
and see, as the view expands,
that there is nowhere else to go
except onwards and upwards
towards the peak which is nowhere
the point where I am, now here.

VIEW

Ripple lines of wavelights
Out to sea, shape into a ship
Sailing slow to shore.

Fine full sails blow like
Winds as white waves
Sweep the prow line
Proudly pointing.

Shining into mist the ship
Becomes the sea, the sky,
The winds that blow.

Man on a hilltop staring seawards
Mist rises in his eyes and out to sea.
He blinks, the ship has sailed on by.
He waits, he watches, unravished
Of the vision, robbed and blank.

Softly in the heats of the plain
A city stirs, a beast asleep,
Smoke rises like a signal,
Noises rear themselves from afar.

He turns to see the place
Of his connection,
Foundry where vision must be forged,
Fired and cut into steel
links of living moments.

Each step of surety and substance
Leads like shining thread
Through the labyrinth of the city,
Out to the harbour's sea-splashed space,
Where the sea-keen eyes of the mariners
Greet him as the ship sails in.

THANK YOU

For all the jewel encrusted,
velvet-stoned cathedrals
and murmuring chants of monks -
all these elaborate mistakes;

For all the lines of poets -
their words strung like stones -
and fine thoughts that swanned
through tired minds at dawn;

For questions of the capstone
that bubbled, sometimes sprung
the surface of troubled times;

And for the vision dipped in night,
renewed each miracle morning
by those who cloistered mystery
in safe hearts.

PRIZIONE

Serene and grave,
The immaculate head
Looks down
On the waves of rough hewn stone
From which its smooth limbs
Seek to arise.

Aphrodite on her shell,
The native on his fragile raft,
Tensile structures of the atom
Ride the currents of the spirit,
Cells that in the bloodstream move
With the swift pulse of power, soft
Cries of the fire that flickers
Fierce in renewing flame.

Serene, benign,
The invisible head
Looks down
On upheavals of the unformed flesh
From which its perfect body
Seeks to emerge.

And newborn man
Looks up
To see his body,
Shaken into place
By the slow beating wings
Of the archangel.

LONDON BRANCH

Chandeliers fall gracefully
Through soft shining space
Stairways curve up
And carpet pours down.

Blue twist of a bannister
Basement bright light bulb
Carpets softly connecting through rooms.

Kettle gleams from the cellar kitchen,
Red electric eye awaiting.
The boss has been shooting
Pheasants hang on hooks in the wall,
Greek coffee smells wrap round the morning.

Shrill telephone bells ring
Through walls, upstairs,
Busy race of the telex chatter
Steady key click typing chatter
Sets the rhythm of the day.

In this busy heaven
Phones ring out into earth,
From a distance through the wires
Carry voices of our foreign legions,
Waves breaking on the surface
Of the deep pile company ocean.

Maps hang picture colours
Charting the invisible,
Papers pile and scatter
Invisible dominion -

Tied fragments of a pipe
That burst somewhere in Oman,
Now sit quiet on our carpet,
Resting after distant perils,
One figure wrong on paper,
One small crack in the PVC
And water mushroomed in the desert sand.

Seasons pass in pictures
As calendar pages turn
(Coloured sheaves of paper
Coloured paper leaves)

Photographs of fields and seas
Reminders of green blue spaces
(Duplicated -
Green flash photocopy)

Refugees of different kinds
Meet here -

Black-winged eyebrows,
A look that's a glare
And all he sees is the Cyprus Isle
Looming large through sun-scaped seas,
Singing like a dark heart beat,
Strong through invisible skies.

JUNGLE

I came from jungle depths
to reach this clearing
at first reluctant -
it was such a tiny space.
I came infrequently
slinking back to jungle haunts
knowing everything was changed.

I loved the jungle.

It was a backdrop
dangerous and exotic context
through which to roam.

Full flowing rivers drop and rush
cascading triangles thrashed into rocks
spray flings up gold against black branches
a nest of seeds, a forest of secrets,
reward of the brave, of the breakers of boundaries,
waterfalling, fairground, sunshafted,
pebbled and grey-banked mud
floating wise-eyed hippopotami.

Jungle night clubs, wild night dancing
under stars
never ending stories wound
like vines around dark spaces,
bright blossoms kissed our limbs and faces
dabbing a cruel and helpless luminosity.

Coffee mornings bleak and rich
beach pounding waves a long way off.
Invisible smoke curls and creepers.

We could dance forever, weaving the vine,
always on the trail, never claiming a goal
riding every mood and change
living for the edge of style.

Shadowed lids peering from our
coffee cups and cocoanuts,
glistening hair curl, eye-brow arch, dancing floors
and the beat goes on and on and on
louder in the night time, quieter by day,
rhythm, rhythm sounding out a jazzy
casual oh so irresistible command.
Jewels, sapphires, stars hung
invisibly stringed from trees
electric on the blackness -
oh the whirl and swirl of the dark river!

The sky we didn't see much
jungle screens filtered white light
tawny jungle green and gold.
Sometimes in open spaces
we came across the sky
large and alien like another planet
dry lion canyons, heavy boulders
piled large, windswept stillness
dusting sand, cliffs calling back
signalling like worn hieroglyphics -
a sky spread bland and without reference,
milky-eyed and cloud cold.

This clearing shows the sky anew
never seen before.

Like a filmset rambling on and on
through some deserted studio
music at times spilled different
scents and trails, lavishly, unlimited.

The set was glamorous as ectachrome
shiny as the silken dreams of night,
papiermache, tinsel -
faded lamp glow in the dawn.

A dimension was always missing -
delight spontaneous the first event
contrived a little in each repeat.

The gifts and prizes and stolen goods
of heartbreak competitions
perilous and lush like rare fruit
strings of disappointments hung
adorning knobbled branches
fretted and wrought with piquant emotions
curled and rippling decorations
not the motion real, the strong pulse
the fierce soft fire stream of love.

The patterns of the jazz hot heart beat
wove quick quick slow in a terrible
slow realised repeat.

We carried ourselves like
interesting exhibits
lounging angular and leopardine,
politely and casually desperate,
some animals made a style
out of glitter -

we were hungry in the jungle
teased our appetites with empty delicacies.

I viewed the clearing from my jungle eerie
jungle music in my ears.
It looked small and tight and white
and barrenly demanding.

A small white circle arrogantly
assuming a focus for the whole
entwined and steaming jungle,
whirl of branch and leaf, vine
and creeper, wild and honeyed
prowl of beasts.
Unimpressed by the tangles and heartbreak
unmoved by the tribal scars and dances,
the strange costumes, sacred customs,
just quietly being a space -
a beginning - sharp, slap morning water
promise of a new beginning!

Now I see the jungle from this clearing
daylight in a smoky room.

Change the world they used to roar
fill it full of jungle tunes, it must improve.
No real aims, just guesswork,
amateur gorilla warfare, fought
in fits and stops, inaccurate
between the cafes and the tropical banks,
and underground in parrot dusky spice bars.

We are never hungry
we are lean.
The craving comes from careless wondering
wandering down forest walks.
The razor edge is here,
no longer just the stylish trimmings,
but the strait and narrow
the absolute connection
straight line from this clearing
through the supermarket jungle
the disneyland of innocent delight
garden blossoming fruit
full and ripe around its core.

Now I love the clearing and the pioneers.
Grudgingly at first -
tugged by jungle connections.
You didn't seem too stylish,
you never quite fitted anywhere
in the jungle, but now I understand,
a terrible tenderness newborn
stemming from that unlocked space inside
saved up but not sealed up forever,
rising tide, a running river
bright out of darkness
birdwing flight across the day.
We follow unashamed the sun
the mists and luxuries of imagination
evaporate like green sickness
in the warm blare, skin seeping
golden spread of the sun.

PHOENIX

What cheap comforts will we seek,
what window glow against the night
and cosy, bright commercial myths
accept and aim for in the grey, vague
jumble of our thoughts, our lives?

Straggling remnant of a world
too bright for clouded memory
too complete to be recorded -
a language that is black and white
can tell us nothing of pure gold.

But underneath layers of the fallen word
beneath the costly grey of compromise
burns still a steady spark of gold.

Only find the wind to fan this
and flames will fire a new world -
from grey ashes of the old,
and fiery, phoenix feathers,
unfold the angel wings of gold.

MICHELANGELO'S DETAIL

That hand stretch
delicate finger touch
across the chapel ceiling,
the ease of perfection
broad outreach of balance.

Oh for that ease in ordinary days
filled with the grandeur
of white limbs flying steady
through strong blue skies.

People stand at the edges of themselves
and shout across at one another,
peering towards the yellow centre
they are discomforted and dazzled.

Fingers touch - the yellow flames
burn hot - keep moving through
to cool blue calm of the core:
blue skies of the Sistine chapel.

And when the hands join - finger touch -
all the bonds are burnt away
symbols dissolve into limitless space
as ceiling turns into sky.

ORDINARY PEOPLE

Ordinary people touch into
the edges of special people's lives.
They know a smudgy bit
about quite a number of things
and avoid the demanding
glamour of extremes.
Their passions, compromised
for so long by the price of houses
and the repeating round
of their daily lives,
seem alien from disuse,
obscured by the long wait
for something significant to happen -
a sign that they can call definite,
to clutch hold of and haul themselves
up to instant and easy salvation.
But even the angel-visited shepherds
had to walk into Bethlehem.

PAST LIVES

Castle encased in its own shadow
Dark against the brilliance of morning blue
A chill radiance on the city buildings
The air is gold, smelted by cold night.
The city grows forest-like and black
On hills and edges, deep crevices
Spill views like streams, issuing
From the dark grey stormy wet stone
Through secret courts and closes down the hill.
Ancient antlers of a church lift against the blue.
And in the painting the stag at the head of the valley
Stares alert as a symbol of the country,
In grey, green, brown and wild waters.

And down from the cobwebby, dark satin
Corners of history, and out of the craggy,
Moor-backed, crofting, ancient-mountained,
Wild stubborn land comes this crowd of people.

A seething hive of bodies
Leading more or less coherent lives
Seeking with their complex patterns
To ignore the absence of a core.
Tenacious cataloguing of the past
        cultivation of the arts
        toleration of the church
To all of which a rushed, bewildered
Reverence is dutifully paid
As if in hope that here the meaning
Somehow lay.

SIMPLICITY

Take off your coloured coat of scars -
Bright embroidery worn with pride,
Stare into the jade-stone flames
Be made new, burnt young again and scarless.

4 Radiance

Pulsation moves through stillness
movement without movement

at the point of intersection
                        intercession
where all movement is
all stillness

joy is acknowledgement of vision
passion the fire of its translation

HOME

100 Mile House, British Columbia
for Valerie and Fred

Dear home,
rough-beamed, beflowered
magnificent, familiar and safe.
I've found you, left you,
longed for you, returned,
outgrown you at last and now
I love you with a four-legged
stable love, the love of home.

Unsung Shangrila
hill-hidden in the north,
behind white winter snows
and the cold world's sorrows.
Shining string of lights
along Alaskan highway -
train whistle western flare
flings echoes of Indians
and evening supper smells.

Ferns dangle down
and steam billows up
inbetween the kitchen floats
green from airy ceilings;
giant dishwasher's steel mouth lifts and shuts
punctuates the doorswing dance
of table layers and cooks.
Land of smells - bread
safe as the history of eating,
warm peach and apricot wrap
ambrosia round the canning room walls.
Pantry prickling with spice and pasta,
honey pails, packets of yeast
and dusty bottled vinegar.

Cool cloak of the walk-in,
sky-high with apples
white-walled, white milk
and crumbly cottage cheese.
Sacks of corn and onions and acid
red tomatoes mix with
left-overs and chocolate cake.
Sweep down the Milky Way
to the blue-bubbled, laced
windowed laundry room,
vats of soap and softeners
and the warm quiet of irons.

Little wooden cabin
growing like a plant
perfumed with coffee
and oven-fresh cakes -
somewhere the vast steppes
are remembered here, on
cossack kicking silver ice;
night joins the world's spaces
the fine spun and familiar past,
man's story through the ages
unwinds with the swirl of
steam from my coffee cup.
And the mirrors are gold framed pictures
of wallpaper flowers in repeat
behind the rows of china plates.

Rare winter wind stirs the night trees,
winds round the cosmos
blowing the green veiled
Northern Lights, shaking out
signs secret as the seasons'
frosty dance around the pole.

Banquet of blunt ritual
clink and cheer of toasting loud and long
from silver goblets.
Comfort careless as a batchelor's room,
defined, content, unfinished,
detail growing hardy amid masculine beams.
Spacious hall of friendship, where our intimacy
holds like leaded glass the light in place.

SUNRISE
Sunrise Ranch, Colorado

Smouldering with purpose
our passion rises from this place
invisible incense on the heated air.

Shock waves of the world roll through here
currents grappling in the agony and
the ecstasy's familiar ebb and flow.
In the rocking, smoking earth
we stand, straddling these waves,
while the flotsam of the ages pours on through
we fling the beached waste upon our altar,
our love burns fiercer than emotion
only gold comes through the flame.

The ocean sky conducts swift storms
clouds, moves and clears to blue,
green waves of the upturned earth
lap around this valley,
quilted with the hissing sprinklers -
dew picked webbing upon the green.

The rough-stoned cave church
conceals fine formed crystal,
rococo soar of the altar piece
dripping candle castles, gilt and glass;
precise chain mail of worship, flowing
glitter of Vivaldi's knitted notes,
holiness cherished in fine-fretted gold.

Click and flow, delicate as clockwork,
mimeographs the distant earthquakes
tender heartbeats of a new born world,
incense scents, we tend
the generations
incantations
songs of praise
heart's prayer.

Subtle as a woman overcoming fear
soft and stubborn, torn and open
yielding into love and strength,
sweet tenderness distilled like
beseeching dew upon the desert earth,
soil soaked red from a stormy past.

Wave upon green wave
grows the garden,
detailed as the dew
begonias in wooden tubs,
dandelion lawns, black tulips
royal by the laundry room,
stream running like a story-
book beneath our windows,
pink daisy heads afloat
upon its tall grass banks,
snowing cottonwood trees
and yellow honey locusts
weight the air with blossom.

A man sits quiet by the flames,
fire speaks to fire,
the passion gold to gold.
Outer petals brush against you,
burn gentle at his passing
incidental supplication -
come into the golden core!

Place of resolution:
night rain and wind
after storms hung
heavy in the afternoon.

Before the massive wisdom of the judge
the peasant woman and the queen
step inside the white chalk circle
and she who loves the most, lets go.

UNTOLD STORIES
for some of the Sunrise dwellers

You
quiet ones

you're the ones
that really
amaze me

I come with
my colourful story
unfolding in well-
shared sagas.

Your stories
are untold
or just fold
into the
background

You're not
too concerned
about it all

You're just
being here

In your presence
I sense the
temple air

your love
your life lived
for this larger life

your communion

in the invisible
and utterly
complete
contentment
of the holy core

And I feel grateful

ENGLAND

Dear England
dear tired land,
stop trying to fall asleep.
Face the world of which you are a part
to which you were a guardian,
discern the role that's needed now.

Like a parent dismayed at
the growth of her children
reluctant to acknowledge
their promise of life
your pretence that nothing
has changed comes back upon you -
you cannot ignore the slowly
unravelling strings of compromise -
change must come,
let it be rebirth,
not a gradual decay.

Bright jewel in the sea,
tiny point
differentiated in Empire,
strings cut one by one,
a net releasing silver fish
and nations -
glad, unbegrudged births.

Legendary holy isle
focus of mystery and power,
your green depths, quest-filled valleys
hold something in trust.
Well loved details and deep roots
that disappear - links to
another state somewhere -
but the connection is now,
the meaning is here.

Morning light and mist
combine in radiance
over your still, chill blue-green moors,
a new breeze stirs the green-leaved grass
fine like hair -
the bones of the earth move
the knights of old stir.

ONENESS

Oneness,
you're probably tired of the word,
a tired word, spoken without substance
many times before.

But you are tired, tired of the hollowness,
ready for something new,
for someone to connect with
not the old, emotional embrace of souls,
but the connection which frees,
acknowledges union, unfathomable, immaculate,
controlled.

You are thirsty, thirsty for the clear stream
that runs deep through mens' hearts
singing nobility and light -
simple and from the core of you
nothing else will do.

And here is oneness
oneness with the source of being,
not a clinging to some one else,
but alignment in oneself, union within
and in that fresh space
you are one already
with everyone
and everything.

WOMAN

I have stood in social gatherings
while my insides caved in
and blackness covered the colour of the evening.
I have stood, quietly amazed,
still chatting
while red pain shot through the black
and my consciousness numbed over
with the fear of loss.

I have lain face down on my bed
with an ache of fear
crumbling like an avalanche inside
while Beethoven played loud
and wondered that the world around
gave no signpost for this
inner vastness of dread
all because someone was late.

My whole body has been catalysed into light
by the expression of a man's face
by the curve of his neck, or the shape of his hand.

I have wanted some one so badly
that I didn't know how to set about living
any kind of life without them.

I have seen God in a man's eyes
and betrayed that recognition
and been tortured with remorse.

I have been horrified
by the nightmarish complexity of my heart
the dense inner workings

I have longed for simple, direct self-expression
innocent, guileless, unashamed.

I have been moved
by the beauty of my deepest vision
and the rich web of essence
through which I receive my world.

And I have learned that the innocence of a woman
is different from that of a child.
A woman's innocence is earned.
She must descend into the underworld
of her own nightmarish heart,
and come back up,
and light the way with her own truth.
And then, burned clean,
she begins to know innocence.

I have known the fear of growing old

the humiliation of compromise

the agony of misunderstanding.

I have known the exultation of breaking limitation

the pride of upright and perfect function

the joy of communion.

I have been appalled at my petty meannesses
my obsessive jealousies
sickened by my lack of vision.

I have known murderous fury at a man's betrayal
devastation in uncovering his childish heart.

And I've grown large enough to understand
wise enough to let it go.

I have been alarmed
at my own capacity for passion
frozen in expression
because there seemed no acceptable means
of release.

I have learned that one has to be brave
to keep the passion moving
to let it out, and not to undersell it.
Never be afraid of your own depth of current!
It must flow, or we lose our radiance,
we feel grief and don't know what's wrong.
Trust your passion, not your analyst.

I have known complete acceptance from a woman,
unconditional love
unquestioning trust
abiding respect.
If I betray that woman, it is because I betray myself.
In honouring and loving her
I know I can honour and love all women.
I can be spacious,
forgiving all affectation, all miasmic views of who I am,
all jealousies and concern about position.
And keep checking my own miasmas.

I have known a love so deep for a man,
that it transcended all demand, all wants
all need of outer assurance.
It didn't matter if I never saw him again.
He was my friend for life.
I found space to breathe
in the stillness and clarity of his presence.
And honouring that connection
I honour all men.
Putting aside manipulation, come ons, put downs,
brashness, falsity and intolerance.

I have known above all
a passion for clarity
for flight
for blue sheer space and light

I have wielded my perceptive heart
like a blue-flamed sword,
cutting away all spurious expression.

And gradually, after much emotional hangover,
and many subconscious minefields
that passion has carried me clear
clear of emotional addiction.
I have become free,
free to be a woman
free to love

And I love other women
their colour, their complexity, their clothes!

I love men, their complementarity
their otherness, their hearts.

And I love being a woman,
being complete
being

PRIESTESS
for Tessa

You are lions and tigers to us
tawny and fierce and tender.

You are deep green oceans to us
bright with coloured fish, alive with
currents of change.

You are a great sun rising in our lives
hot and golden yellow,
burning us and warming us
and making things grow.

Yes, and you are deserts, huge shapes
sculpting in the winds, and levelling back;

You are torrent rivers, silver
in dark, bird-decked forests.

Why seek safe corners when
you offer whole continents to explore?

You are Isis, leaving us in winter
returning in the spring,
after germination in the darkness
compelling new shoots out of wintry ground.

You are Isis, moving always between
dark and lightness, night and day,
cool northern mind, hot-hearted
south, winter and the spring.

Sometimes we have not known where to find you
the entrances to the underworld are many.

We all get caught in our own magic at first,
it is our gift, our door, our weak point
where growth can mushroom through to strength.

And you are thorough in the underworld
summoning up wounded currents out of
earth to be healed in the fire,

Resurrecting loveliness
out of barren social wastelands,
out of parched hard places
in sophisticated woman's heart.

Shaman priestess,
this is a great magic you have worked.

DANCING
for some of the women I know

In a thousand hallos and goodbyes
I know you - on doorsteps,
in trains, at airports, in planes,
in unhappy kitchens, and crowded cafes,
over coffee, over tea, and in grand
collective ceremony.

Sometimes we have lived together,
later we are visiting friends;

Sometimes we share confidences,
then invisible curtains fall
disconcertingly between us.

Space opens up, space closes down:

Everything flows, everything is jagged - ouch!
as we bump into awkward corners
of each other, unused to the touch.

But these days we don't worry so much,
we have learned to trust - yes!
we are learning the dance.

The riddles of our individual lives
are found woven into huge coherence:
wonderful patterns are glimpsed, forming and
dissolving like fireworks in the night;
we feel rhythm, like African drums,
moving under all, and we are ravished
by the beauty of many-faced
Shakti dancing endlessly through us all.

TWO FRIENDS - YIN
for Yujin

Dark
mysterious
moon
eternally moving through stillness

indefinable

a clown
unselfconscious
juggling tennis balls after dinner,
debonair as a filmstar
severe as a leader
compact as a wise man.

A heart
childlike in tenderness
great with passion.

The sudden completeness
of your thought
emerges as from nowhere -
without preliminary steps.

Strong, because you are fully present,
dextrous, because you see far ahead -
the fullness of your presence
and accuracy of aim
inexorably prove out
the true way from the tangent.

A charlatan cannot fool for long
the man of integrity -
no matter how open his heart.

YANG
for Bruce

Golden
upright
sun
honouring always the fire

undeflected

mad and fearless
daring impossible feats,
dashing as a cossack dancer
awesome as a prophet
unbending as a king.

One pointed in passion
your heart is fiery
burning all impurity.

Your clear, deliberate reason
hushes all prefabricated thought.

Your movement is as absolute
and simple as the truth -
to which the world around
conforms, or keeps its distance.

And as the rhythm
of the coming waves
gently pushes change,
your diligence will check it out,
your humour let you move.
The truth is as absolute and simple
as water is unconfined and fluid.

MOUNTAIN LIGHT

This is my view
this outpost here, in the misty hills.

I love this view, this place.

A golden sun
large and rippling strong
pulls out of night
bringing day.

I watch it slow
between the crags
from my place
my view.

A range of half-seen shapes
plays inside - the perception
of light shining through them,
making them known, like
glistening water reflected on rock.

Sometimes they come dancing out -
a procession from the underworld;
sometimes there is just the
turning, the movement
of mist, of unformed waters.

I look down, I look up
it is the same.

Always the sun
large and golden
pulsing with a common beat
lifts up and out of shady hills
into morning.

In the night I am one
I am single
piercing into newness
touching the dark
looking into the
shining eyes
alone, in the blackness,
naming form.

And as the orange disk
wheels up and over
far off mountains
my view fills out
the air sparkles
the earth is content.

Out of the half light
appear figures, others
perched among the cliffs,
watching with me.

Their views are different,
ranges I don't understand
a cast of feature
a look, a way.

But we all watch together
as the sun rises in the sky
we hold a world between us
I am many
I am one.

SUN

I am a sun
flinging flames of radiance

I may seem small
because so far away
but my radiance extends
out of sight.

I am a sun
mysterious and white

clinging to your earthly comforts
you look at me
and do not want to know

for I am that
which you must soon become

another sun

You turn puzzling
about your orbit
wanting me as a setting only
stretching yourself in my warmth

I am a sun
red and hot, dense and light

I see your earthly systems
delicate blossoms
pleasing patterns

but I have solar flares and cycles
and my radiance
extends beyond you
through a universe of worlds

all radiant
all shining
outpouring

this you can only become
you will never grow to like it
understand it

for I am that which
you will soon become

a sun

through the process of
cosmic law

I am turned into that to which I turned
I am that
which all must soon become

I am a sun.

THE SINGLE EYE

Many hanging ends
things unfinished
and undone,

Many private griefs and
doubts, holes in myself
- in my loyalty
- in my stamina.

Anxious, undefined things:
fear that I'll betray,
a sense of incompleteness -
no clues to the pattern.

Only one thing is sure,
one thing always certain -
the bright spot
that's me.

Flame that will always
in the end
have say,
have sway.

Amid the mess
the darkness
I zigzag round
to find the course.

I won't stop
will never stop.

I'll leave behind
coherent surface shapes
all pleasing symmetry
and familiar formulae

To discover, in the dark,
the way,
to always find
at the end of things

The bright spot,
the light,
that's me.

There are no more creeds
and credos
no assuring answers.

We've moved beyond the maps
out on unmarked, open
territory here, subtle,
unknown, the new frontier.

Say nothing, I can say
nothing
can make no further
protestation.

I only know the bright spot
fading to a small point
flaring into flame,
the light, that's me.

SPIDER PLANT

Silent green explosion
From nowhere
Slowly growing
Endlessly

CONTAINMENT

To contain
is not to spill
to have content
to know contentment
to be content

While fires heat up
and container turns
to crucible.

INSIGHTS

Before
the insights
I saw
seemed so
complete
I wrote them monuments.

Now
they come
too thick
and fast
for framing,
small sharp silver blades -

tools for spiritual surgery.

GOD IS NORMAL

I'm beginning to wish
I'd never met you,
I said to God.

Can't you take back my vision -
it's all become such a strain,
please, can't I be normal again?

And all the time I
was feeling so wretched
to even be thinking these things.

Nothing happened for a bit,
till suddenly the thing
switched around in my head:
another dichotomy
doing the flip.

God *is* normal, I thought.

You need intensity,
you need mundanity -
all these dualities,
the warp and the weft of things.

I'm worrying all this time
around a hole - a little
niggling, black hole.
Finally I locate it
and take a look in -
nothing there - in fact
it disappears, becomes a
part of the whole: holy -
you know, normal.

BRIGHT STARS

I came full of brightness and news
and the pattern of my life ready,
like holiday snaps, for showing.

And we talked, me like a neon light
flashing bright its repeating display
in the dark and unassuming night.

Darkness made my colours glow bright
but in the blackness, other currents
stirred, suddenly we had stepped
into a larger pool, deeper waters.

We felt awkward, but as we said
goodnight, we tilted back our heads
and in the cold, thin-aired night
high stars shone oh so bright.

NEW BEARINGS

I love those times
when everything
I think I know
dissolves

When the paving stones
and buildings
of solid assumption
turn suddenly old
and collapse

And I am left newly outside
in the blue shock of the biting air.

The tumbling rush of masonry
has stopped, but dust still flies
in wild gusts of displacement
blurring over the scene.

Later it will settle and clear
and I'll find new bearings:
a wider view, a simpler world.

KNOWING THE FIRE

It wasn't for this -
don't you remember?

It wasn't for all this pettyness,
this strained and awful
state of self-righteousness,
this obsession with role
and all the other trappings
of spiritual bureaucracy.

It wasn't for this pitiful copy
of the fallen human state
that we pledged our hearts
together in the fire.

It wasn't to be better than
one another, to put down,
to subtly undermine.

No, it was to light a
running flame of communion.

Nor were we ever meant
to hide our heads in false
humility, to sit on the most
precious parts of ourselves -
undervaluing them, deferring
always to some one else,
following, sheep-like, the crowd
hoping for safety in numbers.

Nor to pump ourselves up
like ridiculous frogs
with self-importance
notching up progress marks.

And we are not here
to maintain appearances,

but to be brave enough
to reveal ourselves,
and stay with that, never
mind what currents come.

(And don't accept the lie
that honesty means
permission to judge and
condemn, no matter how
cleverly disguised.)

And it wasn't to set ourselves
apart from others, with
careful assessment of
their spiritual credentials.

No, it was to receive into
the fires of our love
everything - trusting
the flames to purify
because that is what we are.

And knowing the fire -
who cares about anything else?

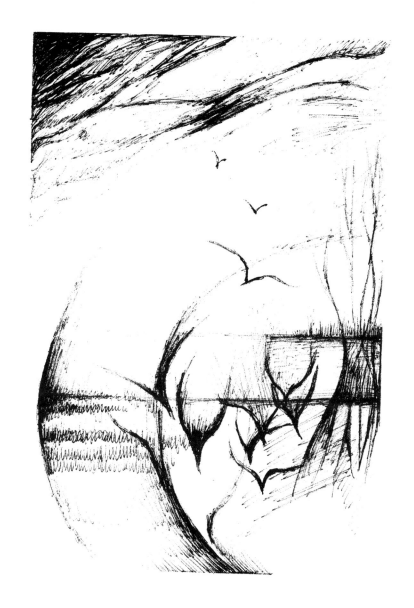

BIRD FLIGHT

From the corner of my eye
I catch a flicker
of bird flight - flung
silver through far air.

A still world,
but sprung sometimes into motion
as we drive,
roadway pouring underneath us
greenness spreading either side;

Green shapes moulded out of grey,

Soft grey light
soft day air
dawn-like

Enshrouds the hills and trees
that loom into dimension
like God's thoughts.

An English day
a brooding heart
a still world
hung soft green
in the grey sky.

The far birds dip and soar

sweet, sweet

Like the deepest breath
taken and released,

Like a sigh
like the deepest sigh

Full, from the heart.

BREATHING FORM
for Jay

1. The Breath

I breathe in the earth
I breathe in the earth

grey black green

green hill backs
sculpt soft
skies
mould grey
rolls

mist floats
hill tops

breath rises

moss damp
dark
bark
brown water
white-foamed
thrown over rock.

Winter trees
reflect in water
turns to black
ripples into
silver
as wind stirs
sun breaks.

everywhere is sacred.

2. Lake

One drop falls
hits
the trembling alive
silver surface
sends out in
circular vibrations
its signal
enlarging outwards
forever across
the water
the whole
universe
turning
towards
oneness
meets and
crosses over
with all the other
circles and
creates a trembling
rippling
rising into
form.

3. Glimpses

A sky
long as forever

wide as continents
wider than thought

mountain-edged in distance

a branch bowed with snow

earth breathing

    earth breathing

an ocean
dancing
wave-flecked into mist

dancing
caressing
intricate coastlines
of island clusters

and at dusk lights float
yellow orange buoys
between blue sea and sky.

4. A Day

A day sad as the
history of poets

sky grey and grey
veils drifting over hill cliffs

a certain sombre feeling
in our hearts
and heaviness

of lives too fiery

of short lives

of brown rivers white-foamed
over rocks

of too much passion

of lives too brief for resolution

beauty too intense to be sustained

Shall we always
I always

walk down this way
this life

with you, together.

RAINBOW LOVE

There are different
     flavours to love

Let us not deceive
     ourselves.

Love is as white as it
     is many-coloured

It is cloud and rainbow
     touching earth.

SONG OF THE UNIVERSE

I love you with
stars and
all archetypal things

Asses milk to bathe in
and great
extravagance of silk

All the essences of the east,
with beauty
and gold-threaded brocade.

Deep, before time
this knowing
links constellations

Thoughts of you
give edge and depth
and definition
to other times and places.

Your presence
like a secret store
of pure delight.

The gentlest touch
is my love
with exquisite care,

This love is want-less
it is source and fountain-
head that feeds itself.

Love between angels
is the loveliest thing.

It is what the whole
universe sings.

STAINED GLASS WINDOWS

Stained glass windows

angels clustered
red wings, green wings,
male and female
white-fleshed radiance
of ecstasy

        illuminated with light
     from without
  love from within

a flame
see-through
and flickering ...

The four beasts
in four little clover-
leaf windows

and the berobed
and serious-faced
apostles
gathered underneath.

And Christ
as always
being there
in the middle

golden-haired this one
arm outstretched
in blessing
always

blue and gold
celtic cross
at his chest

tolerant and
patient -
if this is how you want
to understand me.

Clapham church, Yorkshire Dales

SEA OF GLASS

Sea of glass
mingled with fire

heart of an angel
unstained glass

flecked with fire
letting light through

pure in heart
veined with life

blood of Christ
vine of light

angels can do anything

touch is union
at any fathom
of the ocean

hearts' fusion

the pure in heart
see God in one another

holy communion

bread and blood of life

only separation is profane

muddied waters
only stained glass
lead-veined
keeps things apart.

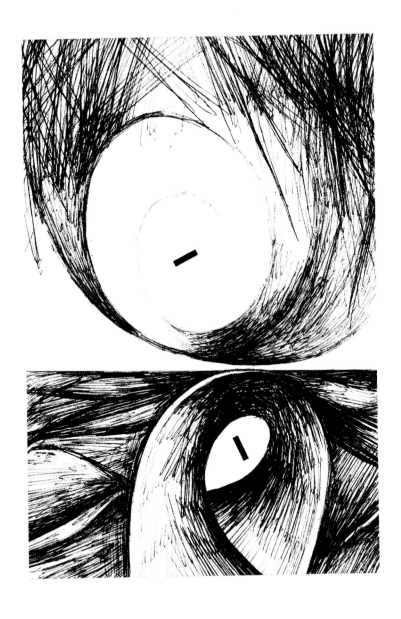

5 The Source

a time of the
ending of cycles
a time of choices
a time to create
to take hold.

you are strong
you are endless
you are love's new song

MANY MANSIONS

If it were not so
I would have told you.

Apparently it is natural
to feel these things

We have not understood
how large love is.

In my Father's house
are many mansions,

If it were not so
we would have been told.

Light breaks

Oh God of ages
I want to find an altar
I want to bow my head

shapes in a life
that seemed broken
and without place

now see them
healed and returning.

seeing you again
I realise how strong I must have grown

The transition from love
                    to   love

I'll do anything for you
except be untrue.

and the pawn became a queen

And there was a sweetness
that burned
and cooled

and a sudden ending of pain
and the sense that true love
could run straight again

the gate of the garden opened
and all that went before
seemed like a strange dream.

And they shall not hurt nor destroy
in all my holy mountain

God of ages
living God

your bright love runs
like fire in my veins

I shall not hurt nor destroy
in all my holy mountain.

Holy mansions
sourced in love.

Invisible curve of current
unique to us, wordless
requiring all I am

sweet sense of belonging
fusion cloud, fire seam
from which we issue

rooted warmth of love shared
daily, strong growing trunk
and branches of our life

strange electric pull, flickering
across the space between
fiery precision of love

light-hearted, delicate space
light-sculpted, potent and
careful sensing of connection

communion beyond desire
the common eye to see things
shared without definition

A universe of love
turning in to oneness
and out in the infinite
colours of our connections

This is how we know the Father
Love God love one another.

Heaven is huge

each mansion sacred,
safe

Out of the Father's house
the root and wellspring
well being
of ourselves

If it were not so
I would have told you.

THE RETURN OF LOVE

1

And the phone rang like a heart beat
into the space

fear rang like a pulse
within the darkness

and he wasn't in
and he didn't answer

and he wasn't in
and he didn't answer

In the deep of my pain
I saw the hag

Saw her, saw me, the hag

gradually encrusting over me
like age

hardening the tenderness of me

stopping up the wellspring of me

masking over the beauty of me

she turned and looked towards me
and then disintegrated in the flame.

2

I love you
I love you
I love you

That's enough

I've always loved you

You may be
a fallen angel

but I love the fire of your life
                    your lust

I know the wild, desolation way
you believe in

You are my fallen angel
Jekyll and Hyde.

This fire burns up
the constructs of my mind

destroying space and time

taking me back to the source

confirming love.

3

Now is the time
of the most delicate
pushing up

of the most tender
unfurling

the time of the return of love

when the fig tree
putteth forth leaves

now is the time
spring time

Up, past the influences
of corruption
and twisted places

up, up to the source
and down to the roots

of new beginning.

4

There are times
when you can feel the pain
of people, of the planet
it's palpable
it screams at you.

Times when it seems too
unbearable to remain
in this constricted skin
just too much to contain.

You can feel it
rising up in waves
like an old burn
re-activated.

No wonder
everyone is addicted
with all this pain
around

gods of comfort
the hard drugs and the soft
like television and
magazines full of glossy
nothing and gossip
and vicarious intrigue
and making it and
houses and children
and illnesses
and cheap sex
and all the games

to keep from seeing
from remembering
from *feeling* the pain.

5

for Jon

at times when I feel like this
empty and blank
unshaped

a crust, a nothingness
afloat on the surface
too light to sink.

I think of you
long to be with you
if you are not close.

Our passion is the passion
of a life lived together

shared daily

small details of home enjoyed
arguments, and all the difficult bits

Sometimes I've wanted to show you other things

but, this is our mansion
it is the mansion in which we live.

When I just need to float
on the surface
in this grey world
dawn-break world

sea not separated yet
from sky

no earth

like a lost girl

just let me be

and in your kindness
which is like a magic
broken bits are mended

in the clear simplicity
of innocence

new beginnings shoot.

BLACK STREAM

and the darkness
under the bridge

black silver
of the stream
the fairytale trees

and the darkness
and the depth
like huge
encircling wings
arose
wrapped around us

infused us

and the depths
and the black floors
of oceans

and deeper

to the unformed
flow of us.

Let me never become
too well-known
a character
glittering
personality
someone who
behaves thus and so
over-defined
cut off then
from my
source

dry

I will always stay
close, deeply
rooted in the
unknown
unnamed
essence
bright dark
mystery
newly pouring
flow of who
I am

RIVER TO THE SEA

1 Highlands

Tartan-clad
plaid hills
in shadow
hills in sun

Clouds float in
and out of lochs
and skies and glens

Clouding grey
clearing to blue and green

Out of the dark north
flows a black spring

(green-eyed, the lion in the north)

We have seen the stream
and now we know its source.

Dark water into glassy green
Flowing south to sun and ocean.

2 Cornish Beach

I will come to this beach
when my body is old

This emerald ocean
shading into royal
blue, navy blue, white-flecked

Lace-edged surf stretching out
and glittering back, hard
gold feet-sculpting sand,

Those endless patterns of
mussel-encrusted rocks and
tidal throw of pebble lines.

The brutal huge cracked and
beaten cliff caves yawning
with the elemental flow

Of tide washing in and out
through ages, through history
through grief and anger, love and longing.

This beach coastline roaring
faintly into blue
distance in the west,

This beach, waves racing huge
in the bay as we come down
the hill, beat of green surf

on hard sand, and I will
come here, like migrating birds
to summer lands,

And this place will be glistening
like a source, and my memories
of times before will pull

Stronger, times when we
never aged, never died
were never born.

3 Regeneration

And the river reaches the sea

That which was lost
has been found

Where there was darkness
where there was doubt
there is love

And the new wave of us
we will not be trapped

All is not lost
nothing has been lost

We are still here
love is still the source

Ecstasy generation
the bravery to be there

And the green sea
turning into turquoise
glittering like jewels
green glass emerald ocean

washing away the doubts
and tiredness

The winds blow
we do not grapple
we are coming through.

ACKNOWLEDGEMENTS

'Tomorrow's Sea' first appeared in *The Pen* magazine, Spring 1986; 'The Pyramid' in *First Time* magazine, No 11 Autumn 1986; 'England' in *Integrity International* magazine in December 1978.

44 of these poems appeared in an initial edition *Fire Path* (Foundation House 1989).

'Sunrise' and 'Simplicity' are in process of being recorded on a C60 cassette tape as part of a compilation of poems, songs and music with members of the Angels of Fire and friends. 'Sea of Glass' is also in process of being recorded on the same tape as a collective piece.

Jay Ramsay, founder of Angels of Fire, edited this book in collaboration with the author.

Thanks to Catherine Smedley for the beautiful drawings.

Thanks also to Kathleen Strnad, fellow poet, who was a catalyst.

More thanks to Andy for help with the typesetting.

Other titles available from The Diamond Press:

JOURNEY TO THE EDGE OF LIGHT- Selected Poems 1965-1985   GEOFFREY GODBERT
86pp Illustrated £4.50 Paperback ISBN 0 948 684 03 8

Drawn from twenty years' work, since his meetings with The Group in the '60's to his involvement with the Greville Press and the Angels of Fire collective in the '80's, this volume traces an evolving personal history, including his long poem 'The Brooklyn Bridge'.

FIRST THINGS   LIZZIE SPRING
99pp Illustrated by the author £4.75 Paperback ISBN 0 94 8684 01 1

Co-founder of the West Country group The Badger Poets, Lizzie Spring combines her gift as a poet with piano composition and performance , and is a member of the Angels of Fire collective. This, her first collection, reflects across her life experience from childhood and young womanhood in a growing preoccupation with the expression of transpersonal values.

THE GREAT RETURN:
THE OPENING/KNIFE IN THE LIGHT - a stage-poem/THE HOLE
(the first three books)
226pp Illustrated £7.95 Paperback ISBN 0 984684 02 X
IN THE VALLEY OF SHADOW-a cine-poem-cum-fantasy/DIVINATIONS
(books 4 & 5)   JAY RAMSAY
373pp Illustrated £9.95 Paperback ISBN 0 984684 04 6

Pioneer of Angels of Fire, editor of *The Third Eye*, and author of *Psychic Poetry - a manifesto* (Diamond Press). The first five books of this major work-in-progress are published complete in two volumes for the first time. In them Jay Ramsay maps out poem by poem an extensive experiential journey through the psyche, in a quest through the dark night of the late 20th Century soul that builds towards life, light and resurrection.

Enquiries : The Diamond Press, 5 Berners Mansions Street, 34-6 Berners Street, London W1P 3DA

Other titles available from Foundation House Publications:

MAGIC AT OUR HAND NANCY ROSE EXETER

136 pp Drawings by the author £6.50 Paperback ISBN 0 935 427 15 5

A collection of meditational essays and poems stemming from the personal wisdom and experience of the author. Magic is at our hand as we become more aware of the invisible aspects of ourselves . The ways in which we interact with others, both intimately and professionally, how we view ourselves, the means by which we source the correct direction for our lives and give expression to our deepest desires and compulsions - are what this book is about.

BEYOND BELIEF - Insights to the way it is
LORD EXETER

200pp £5.95 Paperback ISBN 0 935427 13 9

For over 30 years Lord Exeter served as an example of some one who lived from a new place, a deeper source of identity. These essays, drawn from extemporaneous talks, speak of this dimension , and outline straightforward ways in which others can learn to move beyond belief into a new experience of living.

Foundation House Publications is the publishing arm of the Emissary Foundation International. (See over.)

The Emissary Foundation International conducts public meetings, conferences, seminars and study courses that provide forums in which the individual is assisted to go beyond the limitation of separation and come into an experience of alignment with the inherent rhythms of life.

As a worldwide network of people, the Foundation is also concerned with mature collective expression, simultaneously resolving and including the dance of paradox between the requirements of the collective whole, and the compulsions of individual lives.

This vision sees no boundaries.

For further information contact:

Emissary Foundation International
Mickleton House
Mickleton
Chipping Campden
Gloucestershire GL55 6RY

Emissary Foundation International
Foundation House
4817 North County Road 29
Loveland, Colorado 80537
USA